THE CLOSE LEVEL SELLING:

Unlocking Success in Sales Through Effective Closing Technique

By Asher Bennett

All rights reserved. No part of this publication may be reproduced, distributed, or transmitted in any form or by any means, including photocopying, recording, or other electronic or mechanical methods, without the prior written permission of the publisher, except in the case of brief quotations embodied in critical reviews and certain other noncommercial uses permitted by copyright law.

Copyright © (Asher Bennett), (2024).

TABLE OF CONTENTS

The Importance of Closing in Sales

Understanding The Sales Process

The Psychology of Closing

Building Trust and Credibility with Clients

Identifying Buyer Signals

Overcoming Objections with Confidence

Timing the Perfect Close

Essential Closing Techniques for Every Salesperson

Customising Your Approach for Different Client Types

The Role of Communication in Effective Closing

Handling Rejections and Turning Nos into Yeses

Leveraging Technology to Improve Closing Rates

Case Studies of Successful Sales Closings

Measuring and Improving Your Closing Success

Developing a Continuous Improvement Mindset

Elevating Your Sales Career Through Masterful Closing

The Importance of Closing in Sales

In the fast-paced world of sales, closing a deal is often seen as the pinnacle of the process. It's the moment when all the hard work, relationship-building, and strategic planning come to fruition. However, closing is more than just the final step; it's a critical skill that determines the success or failure of any sales endeavor. To fully grasp the importance of closing, it's essential to understand its role in the sales process, the techniques involved, and how mastering this skill can significantly impact a salesperson's career and the overall success of a business.

Understanding the Sales Process

The sales process is a series of steps designed to guide a potential customer from initial awareness of a product or service to making a purchase decision. These steps typically include prospecting, qualifying leads, presenting the product or service, handling objections, and, finally, closing the sale. Each step is vital in its own right, but closing is arguably the most critical because it's where the deal is either won or lost.

Without a successful close, all the previous efforts—identifying the right prospects, engaging with them, and addressing their needs—can go to waste. The close is the culmination of all the time and effort invested in the sales process. It's where value is realized, and revenue is generated. For this reason, understanding and mastering the art of closing is paramount for any salesperson who wishes to excel in their field.

The Psychological Aspect of Closing

Closing a sale is as much about psychology as it is about technique. Understanding the buyer's mindset is crucial to effectively closing a deal. Buyers go through a psychological journey during the sales process, starting from awareness to interest, then to consideration, and finally to decision. At each stage, the salesperson must address the buyer's concerns, build trust, and reinforce the value of the product or service.

When it comes to closing, the buyer is at a crossroads—they must decide whether to move forward with the purchase or walk away. This decision-making process is often accompanied by a mix of emotions, including excitement, fear, doubt, and anticipation. A skilled salesperson understands these emotions and knows how to address them to guide the buyer towards a positive decision.

For example, fear of making a wrong decision can be a significant barrier to closing a sale. A good closer will acknowledge this fear and provide reassurance by highlighting the benefits, success stories, or guarantees associated with the product or service. They'll also create a sense of urgency, subtly pushing the buyer to make a decision by emphasizing limited-time offers or the risk of missing out on the opportunity.

Techniques for Effective Closing

There are numerous closing techniques, each suited to different types of sales situations and buyer personalities. Here are some of the most commonly used techniques:

1. The Assumptive Close: This technique involves assuming that the buyer has already decided to purchase and proceeding with the next steps, such as filling out paperwork or setting up a delivery date. It's a subtle way of moving the sale forward without explicitly asking for the order.

2. The Summary Close: In this approach, the salesperson summarizes the key benefits and features that the buyer has expressed interest in. By recapping the positive aspects of the product or service, the salesperson reinforces the buyer's decision and makes it easier for them to say yes.

3. The Urgency Close: This technique involves creating a sense of urgency by offering a limited-time discount, a bonus, or the risk of the product being sold out. The goal is to encourage the buyer to act quickly to avoid missing out on a good deal.

4. The Alternative Close: Here, the salesperson presents the buyer with two or more options, all of which lead to a purchase. For example, "Would you like the product in red or blue?" or "Would you prefer the basic package or the premium package?" This technique shifts the focus from whether to buy to what to buy.

5. The Direct Close: Sometimes, the best approach is to be straightforward. The direct close involves simply asking the buyer for their business, such as "Can I place your order today?" This technique works well when the salesperson has established strong rapport and trust with the buyer.

6. The Trial Close: The trial close is a way of gauging the buyer's readiness to commit without applying too much pressure. It might involve asking a question like, "How does that sound to you?" or "Is this what you're looking for?" Based on the buyer's response, the salesperson can either move towards closing or address any remaining concerns.

The Impact of Mastering Closing Skills

Mastering the art of closing has a profound impact on a salesperson's success. Not only does it lead to higher conversion rates and increased revenue, but it also builds confidence and fosters long-term relationships with clients. A salesperson who can consistently close deals is more likely to be seen as a trusted advisor rather than just a vendor, leading to repeat business and referrals.

For businesses, effective closing techniques can lead to a more predictable revenue stream and better financial performance. Companies with sales teams that excel at closing deals are often more competitive in the marketplace, as they can secure more customers and grow their market share. Additionally, closing skills are closely linked to customer satisfaction. A smooth, confident closing process reassures the buyer that they've made the right decision, reducing buyer's remorse and increasing the likelihood of positive word-of-mouth.

Moreover, the ability to close deals effectively is a critical component of career advancement in sales. Top-performing salespeople who consistently meet or exceed their targets are often rewarded with promotions, bonuses, and other incentives. These individuals are also more likely to take on leadership roles within their organisations, where they can mentor others and drive the company's sales strategy.

The Role of Closing in Building Long-Term Relationships

Closing a sale is not just about making a one-time transaction; it's about building a foundation for a long-term relationship with the customer. When done correctly, closing reinforces the value of the product or service and sets the stage for future interactions.

For example, consider a salesperson who sells software solutions to businesses. The closing process might involve not just securing the initial purchase, but also discussing implementation, training, and ongoing support. By addressing these aspects during the close, the salesperson positions themselves as a partner in the customer's success, rather than just a vendor. This approach can lead to upselling opportunities, renewals, and referrals, ultimately driving long-term growth for the business.

The Cost of Poor Closing Skills

On the flip side, poor closing skills can have significant negative consequences. Salespeople who struggle to close deals may experience lower conversion rates, leading to missed opportunities and reduced income. For businesses, poor closing can result in wasted resources, as marketing and lead generation efforts fail to translate into revenue.

In some cases, the inability to close can damage the relationship with the customer. If a salesperson is too aggressive or pushy in their closing attempts, it can lead to buyer discomfort and even cause the buyer to back out of the deal. Conversely, if a salesperson is too passive and fails to ask for the sale, the customer may lose confidence in the product or service and decide to go elsewhere.

A Short Story: The Power of Closing

Let's illustrate the importance of closing with a short story.

John was a young, ambitious salesperson working for a company that sold high-end kitchen appliances. He was passionate about his products and enjoyed meeting potential customers. However, despite his enthusiasm, John struggled to close deals. He would engage customers in lengthy conversations, showcase all the features of the appliances, and answer every question, but when it came time to ask for the sale, he hesitated.

One day, John was working with a couple who were interested in a top-of-the-line refrigerator. They were impressed by the product and seemed ready to buy, but John, nervous about being too pushy, kept the conversation going without asking for the sale. The couple left the store, saying they would think about it.

The next day, John learned that the couple had purchased a similar refrigerator from a competitor. Frustrated, he sought advice from his mentor, Sarah, an experienced salesperson known for her ability to close deals.

Sarah listened to John's story and then said, "John, you did everything right up until the end. The couple was ready to buy, but you didn't guide them to the finish line. Closing isn't about being pushy; it's about helping the customer make a decision they already want to make. You need to have the confidence to ask for the sale."

Determined to improve, John started practicing different closing techniques. He learned to recognize buying signals and developed the confidence to ask for the order. A few weeks later, he had another opportunity to sell a high-end appliance, this time to a family looking to upgrade their kitchen.

After a thorough demonstration, John noticed the family exchanging glances, a sign that they were ready to buy. He took a deep breath and said, "This refrigerator will be a great addition to your kitchen. Can I arrange for delivery next week?"

The family agreed, and John successfully closed the deal. Over time, he continued to refine his closing skills, and his sales numbers improved dramatically. He realised that closing wasn't just about securing a sale; it was about helping customers make decisions that benefited them and their families.

Conclusion: The Art and Science of Closing

The importance of closing in sales cannot be overstated. It's the critical step where all the efforts of the sales process come together to achieve the desired outcome—a successful sale. Closing is both an art and a science, requiring a deep understanding of human psychology, effective communication skills, and the confidence to guide buyers towards a positive decision.

Mastering the art of closing not only leads to higher sales and increased revenue but also builds long-term relationships with customers, enhances career prospects, and contributes to the overall success of a business. For salespeople who aspire to excel in their field, developing strong closing skills is not optional—it's essential.

In the end, closing is about more than just making a sale; it's about creating value for the customer and building a foundation for future success. By understanding the importance of closing and honing this critical skill, sales professionals can unlock new levels of achievement and secure their place as leaders in their industry.

Understanding The Sales Process

The sales process is the backbone of any successful sales strategy, providing a structured approach that guides potential customers from initial awareness to final purchase. Whether you're selling a product, a service, or even an idea, understanding the sales process is crucial for achieving consistent results and building lasting relationships with your customers. This essay will delve into the various stages of the sales process, the importance of each step, and how mastering this process can lead to increased sales and long-term success.

The Significance of a Structured Sales Process

A structured sales process offers several benefits to both salespeople and businesses. First, it provides a clear roadmap that helps sales professionals stay organized and focused. By following a defined sequence of steps, salespeople can ensure they cover all necessary bases, reducing the likelihood of missed opportunities or overlooked details.

Secondly, a structured process allows for better tracking and measurement of sales activities. By understanding where prospects are in the sales funnel, sales managers can identify areas for improvement and optimize their strategies accordingly. This leads to more accurate forecasting, better resource allocation, and ultimately, higher conversion rates.

Lastly, a well-defined sales process helps build trust and rapport with customers. When salespeople consistently follow a structured approach, customers feel more confident in their decision-making process, knowing that they are being guided by a professional who understands their needs and can provide appropriate solutions.

The Stages of the Sales Process

The sales process typically consists of several key stages, each with its own objectives and strategies. While the specifics may vary depending on the industry, product, or service, the following stages are generally applicable across most sales environments:

1. Prospecting
2. Qualifying Leads
3. Initial Contact
4. Needs Assessment
5. Presentation
6. Handling Objections
7. Closing the Sale
8. Follow-Up

Each of these stages plays a critical role in moving prospects closer to a purchase decision. Let's explore each stage in more detail.

1. Prospecting

Prospecting is the first stage of the sales process, and it involves identifying potential customers who may be interested in your product or service. The goal of prospecting is to create a pool of leads that can be nurtured and moved through the sales funnel.

Prospecting can take many forms, including cold calling, networking, social media outreach, email campaigns, and more. The key to successful prospecting is targeting the right audience—those individuals or businesses that have a genuine need for what you offer. By focusing on quality leads rather than quantity, salespeople can increase their chances of converting prospects into customers.

Effective prospecting requires research and preparation. Salespeople must understand their target market, including the pain points, challenges, and goals of potential customers. They should also be familiar with the competition and how their product or service stands out in the market. This knowledge allows salespeople to tailor their approach and communicate the unique value of their offering from the outset.

2. Qualifying Leads

Once prospects have been identified, the next step is to qualify them. Not all leads are created equal, and qualifying is the process of determining which leads are most likely to convert into paying customers. This involves assessing whether a prospect has the need, budget, authority, and timing (often referred to as BANT) to make a purchase.

Qualifying leads is crucial because it helps salespeople focus their efforts on the most promising opportunities. By filtering out leads that are unlikely to result in a sale, salespeople can allocate their time and resources more effectively, increasing their overall productivity and success rate.

There are several ways to qualify leads, including direct conversations with prospects, conducting online research, or using lead scoring tools that assign a numerical value to each prospect based on specific criteria. The goal is to identify those leads that have the highest potential to move forward in the sales process.

3. Initial Contact

The initial contact is the first direct interaction between the salesperson and the prospect. This stage is critical because it sets the tone for the rest of the sales process. A positive first impression can open the door to further discussions, while a poor introduction can close it just as quickly.

During the initial contact, the salesperson's primary objective is to establish rapport and build trust with the prospect. This involves introducing themselves and their company, explaining the purpose of the conversation, and asking open-ended questions to learn more about the prospect's needs and challenges.

It's important for salespeople to be genuine and empathetic during this stage. Rather than jumping straight into a sales pitch, they should focus on understanding the prospect's perspective and demonstrating that they are there to help, not just to sell. This approach helps build credibility and lays the foundation for a productive relationship.

4. Needs Assessment

The needs assessment stage is where the salesperson delves deeper into the prospect's situation to identify their specific needs, pain points, and objectives. This stage is crucial because it allows the salesperson to tailor their pitch and recommendations to the prospect's unique circumstances.

During the needs assessment, the salesperson should ask probing questions to uncover the underlying issues that the prospect is facing. This may involve exploring their current solutions, the challenges they encounter, and the goals they hope to achieve. The more information the salesperson gathers, the better equipped they will be to present a solution that aligns with the prospect's needs.

Active listening is a key skill in this stage. Salespeople must pay close attention to the prospect's responses, both verbal and non-verbal, to fully understand their concerns and priorities. By showing that they are genuinely interested in helping the prospect solve their problems, salespeople can build trust and position themselves as valuable partners.

5. Presentation

The presentation stage is where the salesperson presents their product or service as the solution to the prospect's needs. This is the stage where all the information gathered during the needs assessment comes into play. The presentation should be tailored to address the specific challenges and goals that the prospect has expressed.

An effective presentation is not just about listing features and benefits; it's about telling a compelling story that resonates with the prospect. Salespeople should focus on how their product or service can solve the prospect's problems, improve their situation, or help them achieve their goals. This may involve demonstrating the product, providing case studies, or sharing testimonials from satisfied customers.

It's also important for salespeople to be clear and concise during the presentation. They should avoid overwhelming the prospect with too much information and instead focus on the key points that are most relevant to the prospect's needs. Visual aids, such as slides or videos, can be helpful in reinforcing the message and making the presentation more engaging.

6. Handling Objections

Objections are a natural part of the sales process, and how they are handled can make or break the deal. Objections may come in the form of concerns about price, doubts about the product's effectiveness, or uncertainty about the timing of the purchase. The key to handling objections is to view them as opportunities rather than obstacles.

When a prospect raises an objection, it's important for the salesperson to remain calm and empathetic. They should listen carefully to the objection, acknowledge the prospect's concern, and ask clarifying questions to fully understand the issue. This demonstrates that the salesperson is genuinely interested in addressing the prospect's needs and is not simply trying to push a sale.

Once the objection is fully understood, the salesperson can respond with a solution or counterargument. This might involve providing additional information, offering a discount, or suggesting alternative options that better meet the prospect's needs. The goal is to reassure the prospect and remove any barriers to moving forward with the purchase.

7. Closing the Sale

Closing the sale is the stage where the salesperson asks the prospect to make a purchase decision. This is often the most challenging part of the sales process, as it requires the salesperson to confidently guide the prospect to a commitment. However, if the previous stages have been executed effectively, closing should feel like a natural progression rather than a high-pressure moment.

There are several closing techniques that salespeople can use, depending on the situation and the prospect's personality. Some common closing techniques include the assumptive close (where the salesperson assumes the sale is already made and proceeds with the next steps), the summary close (where the salesperson summarizes the key benefits and asks for the order), and the urgency close (where the salesperson creates a sense of urgency by offering a limited-time discount or promotion).

Regardless of the technique used, the key to successful closing is confidence and clarity. Salespeople should be clear about what they are asking for and confident in the value of their product or service. They should also be prepared to address any final objections or concerns that the prospect may have.

8. Follow-Up

The sales process doesn't end with the close. Follow-up is a critical stage that involves maintaining communication with the customer after the sale is made. This helps ensure customer satisfaction, address any post-purchase concerns, and lay the groundwork for future sales or referrals.

Follow-up can take many forms, including a thank-you email, a phone call to check in on the customer's experience, or an invitation to provide feedback. The goal is to reinforce the customer's decision, build loyalty, and keep the lines of communication open for future opportunities.

Effective follow-up is not just about making additional sales; it's about building long-term relationships with customers. By showing that they care about the customer's ongoing experience, salespeople can foster trust and encourage repeat business. This stage also provides an opportunity to upsell or cross-sell additional products or services that complement the customer's original purchase.

The Role of Technology in the Sales Process

In today's digital age, technology plays a significant role in the sales process. Sales teams now have access to a wide range of tools and platforms that can enhance their efficiency, improve communication, and provide valuable insights into customer behaviour.

For example, Customer Relationship Management (CRM) systems are widely used to manage and track interactions with prospects and customers. These systems allow salespeople to store important information, such as contact details, communication history, and sales pipeline stages, in one central location. This makes it easier to stay organised and ensures that no leads fall through the cracks.

Automation tools are another valuable asset in the sales process. Sales teams can automate routine tasks, such as sending follow-up emails or scheduling appointments, freeing up time for more strategic activities. Additionally, data analytics tools can provide insights into customer behaviour, helping salespeople tailor their approach and improve their chances of success.

Social media and digital marketing also play a crucial role in prospecting and lead generation. Sales teams can use platforms like LinkedIn, Twitter, and Facebook to connect with potential customers, share valuable content, and build their online presence. Digital marketing campaigns, such as email marketing or targeted ads, can help attract and nurture leads, guiding them through the sales funnel.

While technology offers many benefits, it's important to remember that the human element remains essential in the sales process. Building relationships, understanding customer needs, and providing personalised solutions are tasks that cannot be fully automated. Technology should be seen as a tool that supports the sales process, rather than a replacement for the skills and expertise of sales professionals.

Conclusion: Mastering the Sales Process for Success

Understanding the sales process is essential for any sales professional who wants to achieve consistent success. By following a structured approach, salespeople can stay organized, build stronger relationships with customers, and increase their chances of closing deals. Each stage of the sales process, from prospecting to follow-up, plays a critical role in guiding prospects through their buying journey and ensuring a positive experience.

Mastering the sales process requires a combination of skills, including effective communication, active listening, problem-solving, and the ability to handle objections. It also involves a deep understanding of the customer's needs and the ability to present solutions that align with those needs.

In today's competitive market, sales professionals who can effectively navigate the sales process are more likely to stand out and achieve their goals. Whether you're new to sales or an experienced pro, continuously refining your approach and staying attuned to the evolving needs of your customers will help you succeed in the long run. By understanding and mastering the sales process, you can unlock new levels of achievement and build a rewarding career in sales.

The Psychology of Closing

Closing a sale is more than just a transactional step in the sales process; it is the culmination of a complex psychological journey for both the buyer and the seller. Understanding the psychology behind closing can significantly improve a salesperson's ability to seal deals effectively and build lasting customer relationships. This involves recognizing the emotional and cognitive factors at play, the buyer's decision-making process, and the strategies that can be used to influence that process.

In this essay, we will explore the psychological principles that underpin successful closing, including the role of trust, the power of persuasion, and the impact of emotional triggers. We will also examine some common closing techniques that leverage these principles to guide the buyer toward making a purchase decision.

The Buyer's Psychological Journey

To understand the psychology of closing, it's important first to consider the buyer's psychological journey. This journey is not linear but involves various stages of emotional and cognitive engagement, from initial awareness of a need or problem to the final decision to purchase a solution.

1. Awareness of Need: The buyer's journey begins when they recognize a need or a problem that requires a solution. This awareness might be triggered by external factors (such as an advertisement or a recommendation) or by internal factors (such as dissatisfaction with the current situation). At this stage, the buyer is open to learning about potential solutions but is not yet committed to any particular option.

2. Consideration of Options: Once the need is recognized, the buyer begins to explore different options to address it. They may research various products or services, compare features and benefits, and seek advice from peers or experts. This stage is characterised by a mix of rational analysis and emotional response as the buyer weighs the pros and cons of each option.

3. Evaluation of Risks and Rewards: As the buyer narrows down their options, they enter a phase of evaluating the risks and rewards associated with each choice. This stage is heavily influenced by cognitive biases, such as loss aversion (the fear of making a wrong decision) and the status quo bias (a preference for maintaining the current situation). The buyer's emotions play a significant role here, as they must overcome their fears and doubts to move forward with a purchase.

4. Decision-Making: The final stage of the buyer's journey is the decision-making process. This is where the buyer decides whether to commit to a purchase or walk away. The outcome of this stage is influenced by the buyer's overall experience with the salesperson, their perceived value of the product or service, and their confidence in the decision.

The Role of Trust in Closing

Trust is a foundational element in the psychology of closing. Buyers are more likely to make a purchase when they trust the salesperson and believe that the product or service will deliver on its promises. Building trust involves several key components:

1. Credibility: Salespeople must demonstrate that they are knowledgeable, honest, and reliable. This can be achieved through clear communication, transparency, and consistency in their actions and words. Providing accurate information, answering questions honestly, and avoiding overpromising are essential to establishing credibility.

2. Empathy: Buyers need to feel that the salesperson understands their needs, concerns, and goals. Empathy involves actively listening to the buyer, acknowledging their emotions, and showing genuine interest in helping them find the best solution. By putting themselves in the buyer's shoes, salespeople can build a strong emotional connection that fosters trust.

3. Reliability: Trust is reinforced when the salesperson consistently follows through on their commitments. This includes meeting deadlines, delivering on promises, and being available to address any issues that arise.

Reliability signals to the buyer that they can depend on the salesperson for support, both during and after the sale.

4. Social Proof: Buyers are more likely to trust a salesperson or a product when they see evidence that others have had positive experiences. Social proof can come in the form of testimonials, case studies, or reviews from satisfied customers. By sharing these success stories, salespeople can build credibility and reduce the buyer's perceived risk.

The Power of Persuasion in Closing

Persuasion is a key psychological tool in closing, as it involves influencing the buyer's attitudes, beliefs, and behaviours toward making a purchase. Effective persuasion is not about manipulation but about guiding the buyer toward a decision that aligns with their needs and values. Some of the most powerful principles of persuasion include:

1. Reciprocity: The principle of reciprocity suggests that people feel obligated to return favours or kindnesses. In sales, this can be leveraged by offering something of value to the buyer, such as a free consultation, a helpful resource, or a discount. When the buyer feels that they have received something of value, they are more likely to reciprocate by making a purchase.

2. Commitment and Consistency: People have a natural desire to be consistent in their actions and decisions. Once a buyer has made a small commitment, such as agreeing to a product demonstration or expressing interest in a particular feature, they are more likely to follow through with a larger commitment, such as making a purchase. Salespeople can use this principle by encouraging buyers to take incremental steps toward a final decision.

3. Scarcity: The principle of scarcity is based on the idea that people place higher value on things that are perceived as limited or rare. Salespeople can create a sense of urgency by highlighting limited-time offers, exclusive deals, or the risk of missing out on a popular product. This can motivate buyers to act quickly to secure the opportunity.

4. Authority: People are more likely to be persuaded by individuals who are perceived as experts or authorities in their field. Salespeople can establish authority by demonstrating their knowledge, credentials, and experience. Providing data, research findings, or endorsements from reputable sources can also enhance the salesperson's authority and persuade the buyer to trust their recommendations.

5. Liking: The principle of liking suggests that people are more inclined to buy from someone they like or feel a connection with. Building rapport, finding common ground, and being personable can make a significant difference in closing a sale. When buyers feel a positive emotional connection with the salesperson, they are more likely to respond favourably to their suggestions.

Emotional Triggers in the Closing Process

Emotions play a central role in the buyer's decision-making process, and understanding emotional triggers can be a powerful tool in closing a sale. Emotional triggers are psychological cues that evoke specific feelings or responses in the buyer, influencing their perception of the product or service. Some common emotional triggers include:

1. Fear of Missing Out (FOMO): FOMO is a powerful emotional trigger that can drive buyers to make quick decisions to avoid missing out on a valuable opportunity. Salespeople can leverage this by emphasising the exclusivity or limited availability of a product, creating a sense of urgency that compels the buyer to act.

2. Desire for Belonging: Many buyers are motivated by the desire to belong to a particular group or community. Salespeople can tap into this by positioning their product or service as part of a desirable lifestyle or identity. For example, highlighting how a product is popular among a certain demographic or aligns with a particular value system can make it more appealing.

3. Anticipation of Reward: Buyers are often driven by the anticipation of receiving a reward, whether it's the satisfaction of solving a problem, the pleasure of owning something new, or the pride of making a smart

decision. Salespeople can enhance this anticipation by vividly describing the benefits and positive outcomes that the buyer will experience after making the purchase.

4. Relief from Pain or Discomfort: Many purchase decisions are motivated by the desire to alleviate pain or discomfort. Whether it's a physical pain, such as the need for a more comfortable mattress, or an emotional discomfort, such as anxiety about a work-related problem, salespeople can emphasise how their product or service will provide relief and improve the buyer's situation.

5. Empowerment: Buyers are often motivated by the desire to feel empowered and in control of their lives. Salespeople can appeal to this by framing their product or service as a tool that gives the buyer more power, freedom, or independence. For example, a software solution that streamlines business operations can be positioned as a way to gain more control over time and resources.

Common Closing Techniques

Understanding the psychology of closing allows salespeople to choose the most effective techniques for guiding the buyer toward a purchase decision. Here are some common closing techniques that leverage psychological principles:

1. The Assumptive Close: This technique involves assuming that the buyer has already decided to make a purchase and moving forward with the next steps. For example, the salesperson might say, "Shall I start processing your order?" or "Would you like this delivered on Monday or Tuesday?" The assumptive close works because it bypasses the decision-making stage and subtly nudges the buyer toward a commitment.

2. The Summary Close: The summary close involves recapping the key benefits and features of the product or service that the buyer has expressed interest in. By reinforcing the positive aspects of the offer, the salesperson makes it easier for the buyer to say yes. For example, "You mentioned that you're looking for a solution that's both cost-effective and easy to implement. Our product meets both of those criteria and has a proven track record of success. Shall we move forward?"

3. The Urgency Close: This technique creates a sense of urgency by highlighting a limited-time offer, a pending price increase, or the risk of stock running out. The urgency taps into the buyer's fear of missing out and motivates them to act quickly. For example, "This promotion ends tomorrow, and we only have a few units left in stock. Would you like to secure yours today?"

4. The Alternative Close: The alternative close offers the buyer a choice between two or more options, all of which lead to a purchase. This technique works by shifting the

focus away from the decision to buy and onto the choice of how to buy. For example, "Would you prefer the standard model or the premium version?" or "Should we set up monthly payments or a one-time payment?"

5. The Question Close: The question closely involves asking the buyer a question that prompts them to reflect on the benefits of the product and their readiness to make a purchase. This technique engages the buyer's thought process and often leads to a positive response. For example, "How do you see this solution helping you achieve your goals?" or "What's stopping you from moving forward with this decision?"

Conclusion: Mastering the Psychology of Closing

The psychology of closing is a complex but fascinating aspect of sales that involves understanding the emotional and cognitive factors that drive buyers' decisions. By building trust, using persuasive techniques, and tapping into emotional triggers, salespeople can effectively guide buyers through their decision-making process and close more deals.

Mastering the psychology of closing requires a deep understanding of human behaviour, as well as the ability to adapt one's approach to different buyers and situations. Salespeople who can skillfully navigate the psychological landscape of closing will not only increase their success rates but also build stronger, more meaningful relationships with their customers. In the end, successful closing is about more than just making a sale—it's about creating a positive, satisfying experience for the buyer that leads to long-term loyalty and repeat business.

Building Trust and Credibility with Clients

In any business relationship, trust and credibility are fundamental to success. They serve as the foundation for effective communication, cooperation, and long-term partnership. For sales professionals, consultants, and service providers, building trust and credibility with clients is not just a desirable quality but a critical factor in securing and maintaining business relationships. This essay explores the strategies and principles involved in building trust and credibility with clients, including the importance of integrity, consistency, expertise, and empathy.

The Importance of Trust and Credibility

1. Facilitates Open Communication: Trust fosters an environment where clients feel comfortable sharing their needs, concerns, and feedback. When clients trust their service providers, they are more likely to communicate openly, which allows for better understanding and more effective problem-solving.

2. Enhances Client Retention: Credibility ensures that clients believe in the value of the service or product being offered. When clients perceive a high level of credibility, they are more likely to stay loyal to the business and continue their relationship.

3. Encourages Referrals: Satisfied clients who trust and believe in the credibility of their service provider are more likely to refer others. Word-of-mouth referrals are a powerful source of new business and often come with higher conversion rates.

4. Reduces Sales Resistance: When clients trust a salesperson or consultant, they are less likely to be resistant to sales pitches or negotiations. Trust lowers barriers and opens doors for more effective selling.

Strategies for Building Trust and Credibility

1. Demonstrate Integrity

Integrity is the cornerstone of trust. Demonstrating integrity involves being honest, transparent, and consistent in all interactions with clients. This means:

- Honouring Commitments: Always follow through on promises and commitments. If an issue arises that prevents you from fulfilling a promise, communicate proactively and provide a solution.

- Being Transparent: Clearly explain terms, conditions, and potential issues. Avoid hiding information or making exaggerated claims about your product or service.

- Admitting Mistakes: If an error occurs, own up to it and take responsibility. Acknowledging mistakes and taking corrective actions shows clients that you are trustworthy and committed to resolving issues.

2. Establish Expertise

Credibility is built on expertise and knowledge. Clients are more likely to trust and respect professionals who demonstrate a high level of competence and expertise in their field. This can be achieved by:

- Staying Informed: Keep up with industry trends, advancements, and best practices. Regularly update your knowledge and skills to ensure you provide the most relevant and effective solutions.

- Sharing Knowledge: Offer valuable insights, advice, and recommendations that demonstrate your expertise. This can be done through blog posts, webinars, whitepapers, or direct interactions with clients.

- Showcasing Experience: Highlight your track record of success, case studies, and testimonials from previous clients. Demonstrating your past achievements helps build credibility and reassures clients of your capabilities.

3. Be Consistent

Consistency in behaviour and communication is crucial for building trust and credibility. Clients need to know that they can rely on you to provide a consistent level of service and support. To achieve this:

- Maintain Professionalism: Always approach client interactions with a professional demeanor. This includes being punctual, prepared, and respectful.

- Provide Reliable Information: Ensure that the information you provide is accurate and consistent. Avoid contradictory statements or changing your position without valid reasons.

- Deliver Consistent Quality: Strive to deliver high-quality results consistently. Consistent performance reinforces the perception of reliability and builds confidence in your services.

4. Show Empathy

Empathy involves understanding and addressing the needs and concerns of clients from their perspective. It helps build a strong emotional connection and fosters trust. To show empathy:

- Listen Actively: Pay close attention to what clients are saying and ask clarifying questions to ensure you fully understand their needs and concerns.

- Understand Client Perspectives: Put yourself in the client's shoes and consider their challenges, goals, and expectations. Tailor your approach to address their specific needs and provide relevant solutions.

- Respond Compassionately: Acknowledge clients' feelings and concerns. Show that you care about their well-being and are committed to helping them achieve their objectives.

5. Build Personal Relationships

Building a personal rapport with clients can enhance trust and credibility. Personal relationships create a foundation of mutual respect and understanding. To build personal relationships:

- Engage in Meaningful Conversations: Take time to get to know your clients beyond their business needs. Engage in conversations about their interests, goals, and personal experiences.

- Be Accessible: Make yourself available to clients and respond promptly to their inquiries. Being approachable and responsive reinforces the sense of support and reliability.

- Show Appreciation: Express gratitude for their business and acknowledge their loyalty. Simple gestures, such as thank-you notes or personalized follow-ups, can strengthen the relationship.

6. Provide Exceptional Service

Exceptional service is a powerful way to build trust and credibility. Clients appreciate when their expectations are exceeded, and they are more likely to remain loyal when they receive outstanding service. To provide exceptional service:

- Exceed Expectations: Go above and beyond to deliver value and meet client needs. Look for opportunities to provide additional support or offer enhancements that exceed the client's expectations.

- Solicit Feedback: Regularly ask for feedback to understand client satisfaction and areas for improvement. Act on the feedback to continuously improve your service.

- Be Proactive: Anticipate client needs and address potential issues before they become problems. Proactive service demonstrates foresight and a commitment to client success.

Overcoming Challenges in Building Trust and Credibility

1. Addressing Past Mistakes: If there have been past issues with a client or negative feedback, address them head-on. Acknowledge any past mistakes, explain the steps taken to resolve them, and demonstrate your commitment to improvement.

2. Handling Skepticism: Some clients may approach new relationships with skepticism. Overcome skepticism by consistently demonstrating your commitment to integrity, expertise, and exceptional service. Build credibility gradually through positive interactions and results.

3. Navigating Cultural Differences: In global or diverse markets, understanding and respecting cultural differences is important for building trust. Be mindful of cultural norms and preferences, and adapt your approach to align with the client's cultural context.

Conclusion

Building trust and credibility with clients is essential for long-term success in any professional relationship. By demonstrating integrity, establishing expertise, maintaining consistency, showing empathy, and providing exceptional service, you can create a strong foundation of trust that fosters positive and productive interactions with clients.

The process of building trust and credibility is ongoing and requires continual effort and attention. By committing to these principles and addressing any challenges that arise, you can establish yourself as a trusted and credible professional, leading to stronger client relationships and sustained business success.

Identifying Buyer Signals

In sales, understanding and responding to buyer signals is crucial for successfully guiding prospects through the buying process. Buyer signals are cues that indicate a prospect's level of interest, readiness to purchase, or potential objections. Recognizing these signals allows sales professionals to tailor their approach, address concerns, and close deals more effectively. This essay explores different types of buyer signals, how to identify them, and strategies for responding to these signals to enhance sales success.

Types of Buyer Signals

1. Verbal Signals

   - Questions About Product Features: When a buyer asks detailed questions about product features, specifications, or benefits, it often indicates a high level of interest. For example, asking about the durability of a product or the specifics of its functionality suggests the buyer is considering how the product fits their needs.

   - Statements of Need or Desire: Phrases like "I'm looking for a solution to..." or "This feature is exactly what I need" can signal that the buyer is actively searching for a solution and may be close to making a decision.

   - Objections or Concerns: While objections can initially seem like barriers, they can also be valuable signals. Concerns about price, compatibility, or implementation often indicate that the buyer is evaluating the product seriously and needs reassurance or additional information to move forward.

2. Non-Verbal Signals

   - Body Language: Positive body language, such as nodding, maintaining eye contact, and leaning forward, often signals engagement and interest. Conversely, crossed arms, lack of eye contact, or frequent checking of a watch or phone can indicate discomfort or disinterest.

   - Facial Expressions: Smiles, raised eyebrows, and other positive facial expressions typically reflect interest and satisfaction, while frowns, sighs, or expressions of confusion may suggest doubts or concerns.

   - Physical Actions: Actions such as taking notes, requesting product samples, or asking for a demonstration can indicate that the buyer is actively evaluating the product and is serious about the purchase.

3. Behavioral Signals

   - Engagement with Marketing Materials: How a buyer interacts with marketing materials, such as downloading brochures, attending webinars, or engaging with email campaigns, can provide insights into their level of interest. Increased interaction often signals a higher likelihood of moving forward.

   - Website Activity: Monitoring a buyer's behavior on your website, such as repeated visits to specific product pages or spending time on pricing information, can indicate strong interest and readiness to purchase.

   - Follow-Up Requests: Requests for additional information, proposals, or meetings are strong signals that the buyer is considering the purchase and is looking for more details to make an informed decision.

4. Purchasing Signals

   - Inquiries About Pricing: Questions about pricing, discounts, or payment terms often suggest that the buyer is evaluating the financial aspects of the purchase and is closer to making a decision.

   - Request for Contract or Agreement: When a buyer asks to see a contract or formal agreement, it typically indicates that they are serious about proceeding and want to finalize the details.

   - Timeframe for Decision: Discussions about timelines, such as asking about delivery dates or implementation schedules, can signal that the buyer is planning to make a decision soon and is considering the practical aspects of the purchase.

How to Identify Buyer Signals

1. Active Listening

   - Pay Attention to Details: Listen carefully to what the buyer says and how they say it. Look for hints in their language, tone, and questions that reveal their level of interest or concerns.

   - Ask Open-Ended Questions: Engage the buyer in conversations that encourage them to share more about their needs, preferences, and decision-making process. This can provide valuable insights into their readiness to purchase.

2. Observe Body Language

   - Look for Positive Indicators: Watch for signs of engagement, such as leaning forward, nodding, or smiling. These signals often indicate interest and willingness to proceed.

- Identify Negative Cues: Be aware of signs of discomfort or disengagement, such as crossed arms, lack of eye contact, or fidgeting. Addressing these cues can help resolve objections and improve the buyer's experience.

3. Analyze Behavioral Data

   - Track Interactions: Use CRM and analytics tools to monitor how the buyer interacts with your content, website, and communications. Patterns of behavior can reveal their level of interest and intent.

   - Evaluate Engagement Metrics: Assess metrics such as email open rates, click-through rates, and time spent on product pages to gauge the buyer's level of engagement and interest.

4. Follow-Up and Clarify

   - Seek Confirmation: If you suspect a buyer is ready to move forward but are unsure, ask clarifying questions to confirm their intent. For example, "Based on our discussion, it seems like this solution aligns with your needs. Are you ready to proceed with the next steps?"

   - Address Concerns: If a buyer expresses concerns or objections, address them promptly and provide additional information or solutions to help them feel more comfortable with their decision.

Strategies for Responding to Buyer Signals

1. Tailor Your Approach

   - Customize Your Pitch: Based on the signals you've identified, tailor your sales pitch to address the buyer's specific needs, preferences, and concerns. Highlight features or benefits that align with their interests and provide solutions to any objections they may have.

   - Provide Relevant Information: Offer additional information, demonstrations, or samples that address the buyer's questions and concerns. This can help reinforce their confidence in the product and facilitate the decision-making process.

2. Build Rapport

   - Enhance Personal Connection: Strengthen your relationship with the buyer by showing genuine interest in their needs and concerns. Building rapport can increase trust and make the buyer more comfortable with the purchasing decision.

- Acknowledge and Validate: Acknowledge the buyer's feelings, concerns, and objections. Validating their perspective helps build trust and demonstrates that you understand their position.

3. Create a Sense of Urgency

   - Highlight Limited Availability: If appropriate, emphasize any time-sensitive aspects of the offer, such as limited stock, promotional discounts, or upcoming changes in pricing. Creating a sense of urgency can motivate the buyer to act quickly.

   - Set Clear Next Steps: Provide a clear path forward, including specific actions, timelines, and expectations. This helps guide the buyer toward making a decision and facilitates the closing process.

4. Offer Support and Reassurance

   - Provide Ongoing Support: Offer additional support, resources, or consultations to address any remaining questions or concerns. Ensuring that the buyer feels supported throughout the process can increase their confidence in making a purchase.

   - Reinforce Value: Continuously emphasize the value and benefits of the product or service. Reassure the buyer that they are making a sound decision by highlighting how the solution meets their needs and delivers positive outcomes.

Conclusion

Identifying and responding to buyer signals is a critical skill in sales that can significantly impact the success of closing deals. By recognizing verbal, non-verbal, behavioral, and purchasing signals, sales professionals can gain valuable insights into the buyer's level of interest and readiness to make a purchase.

Effective sales strategies involve tailoring your approach based on these signals, building rapport, creating a sense of urgency, and providing support and reassurance. Mastering the art of identifying and responding to buyer signals not only improves your chances of closing deals but also enhances the overall buyer experience, leading to stronger relationships and long-term success in sales.

Overcoming Objections with Confidence

Objections are a natural part of the sales process and should be viewed as opportunities rather than setbacks. Successfully overcoming objections requires confidence, preparation, and a strategic approach. This essay explores effective strategies for handling objections, including understanding their nature, employing active listening, providing tailored responses, and maintaining a positive mindset. By mastering these techniques, sales professionals can turn objections into stepping stones toward closing deals and building lasting customer relationships.

Understanding the Nature of Objections

1. Types of Objections

- Price-Related Objections: Concerns about cost or budget constraints are among the most common objections. Buyers might feel that the product or service is too expensive or not worth the investment.

- Value-Based Objections: These objections arise when buyers question the perceived value or benefits of the product or service. They might be uncertain about whether the solution will address their specific needs or deliver the promised results.

- Competitor Comparisons: Buyers may compare your offering with those of competitors, raising objections based on perceived advantages or disadvantages of alternative solutions.

- Timing and Urgency: Objections related to timing or urgency can occur when buyers believe they are not ready to make a decision or need more time to evaluate their options.

- Trust and Credibility: Concerns about the reliability or credibility of the product, service, or salesperson can also lead to objections. Buyers might question the legitimacy of claims or the credibility of the source.

2. The Psychology Behind Objections

Objections often stem from the buyer's need for reassurance and certainty. They may arise from fear of making a wrong decision, uncertainty about the product's effectiveness, or concerns about the financial impact. Understanding the psychological motivations behind objections helps sales professionals address them effectively and build trust with the buyer.

Strategies for Overcoming Objections

1. Active Listening

- Hear the Buyer Out: Allow the buyer to express their concerns fully without interrupting. Demonstrating that you are actively listening builds rapport and shows that you respect their perspective.

- Acknowledge Their Concerns: Show empathy by acknowledging the validity of their objections. Phrases like "I understand your concern about the cost" or "It's completely reasonable to have doubts about the product's effectiveness" validate their feelings and create a foundation for addressing their concerns.

- Clarify and Probe: Ask follow-up questions to gain a deeper understanding of the objection. For example, "Can you tell me more about what specifically concerns you about the price?" This helps uncover the root cause of the objection and provides insights into how to address it.

2. Provide Tailored Responses

- Address Specific Concerns: Tailor your response to the specific objection raised. For price objections, provide a detailed breakdown of the cost and highlight the value or return on investment. For value-based objections, offer examples or case studies that demonstrate how the product has successfully met similar needs.

- Compare and Differentiate: If the objection involves competitor comparisons, emphasize the unique features or advantages of your product that differentiate it from alternatives. Highlighting what sets your offering apart can help shift the focus back to its strengths.

- Offer Solutions: Present solutions to the objection that align with the buyer's needs and constraints. For example, if timing is an issue, offer flexible payment options or a phased implementation plan to address their concerns.

3. Maintain a Positive Mindset

- Stay Calm and Confident: Approach objections with a positive attitude and confidence in your product or service. A calm demeanor reassures the buyer and helps maintain a constructive dialogue.

- Focus on Solutions: Instead of dwelling on the objection, shift the conversation toward finding solutions. Emphasize how your product or service can address their needs and overcome the concerns they've raised.

- Reframe the Objection: Reframe the objection as an opportunity to provide additional value or clarification. For example, if a buyer is concerned about the product's complexity, frame it as an opportunity to demonstrate how easy it is to use or how comprehensive the support is.

4. Build Trust and Credibility

- Showcase Success Stories: Share testimonials, case studies, or success stories that address similar objections. Demonstrating how other clients have overcome similar concerns can build credibility and reassure the buyer.

- Be Transparent: Provide clear and honest information about the product, service, or pricing. Transparency helps build trust and reduces skepticism, making it easier to address objections effectively.

- Demonstrate Expertise: Leverage your knowledge and expertise to address objections with confidence. Providing well-reasoned explanations and evidence can help persuade the buyer and reinforce your credibility.

5. Practice and Preparation

- Anticipate Common Objections: Prepare for common objections by developing responses in advance. Practicing these responses helps you address objections smoothly and confidently during sales conversations.

- Role-Play Scenarios: Engage in role-playing exercises to simulate objection-handling scenarios. This practice helps improve your ability to respond effectively and build confidence in managing objections.

- Seek Feedback: After handling objections, seek feedback from colleagues or mentors to identify areas for improvement. Continuous learning and adaptation help refine your approach and enhance your effectiveness.

Conclusion

Overcoming objections with confidence is a critical skill in the sales process that requires active listening, tailored responses, a positive mindset, and the ability to build trust and credibility. By understanding the nature of objections, employing effective strategies, and preparing in advance, sales professionals can address concerns constructively and guide buyers toward making informed decisions.

Handling objections is not just about overcoming barriers but about building stronger relationships with clients. By addressing objections thoughtfully and demonstrating a genuine commitment to solving their problems, sales professionals can enhance their credibility, foster trust, and ultimately achieve greater success in closing deals.

Timing the Perfect Close

In sales, closing a deal at the right moment is crucial for maximizing success. Timing the perfect close involves recognizing when a buyer is ready to make a decision and seizing that opportunity to finalize the sale. Misjudging the timing can result in missed opportunities, while closing at the right moment can significantly increase the likelihood of a successful transaction. This essay explores the factors influencing the timing of the perfect close, strategies for identifying the right moment, and best practices for executing a successful close.

Factors Influencing the Timing of the Perfect Close

1. Buyer Readiness

- Interest and Engagement: The level of interest and engagement shown by the buyer is a key indicator of readiness. If a buyer is actively seeking information, asking detailed questions, and showing enthusiasm, they may be approaching a decision point.

- Decision-Making Process: Understanding the buyer's decision-making process and timeline helps gauge readiness. If the buyer has indicated a specific timeframe for making a decision or has completed necessary evaluations, they may be ready to close.

- Budget and Approval: Confirming that the buyer has the necessary budget and internal approvals in place is essential for timing the close. Addressing any financial or approval-related concerns before attempting to close ensures a smoother process.

2. Sales Cycle Stage

- Discovery Phase: During the discovery phase, the focus is on understanding the buyer's needs and pain points. Timing the close is premature at this stage as the buyer is still gathering information and evaluating options.

- Consideration Phase: In the consideration phase, the buyer is evaluating different solutions and comparing options. Signs of serious interest, such as requesting detailed proposals or product demonstrations, indicate that the buyer may be nearing the decision stage.

- Decision Phase: The decision phase is the most opportune time for closing. The buyer is ready to make a purchase decision and is likely evaluating final details, negotiating terms, and seeking reassurance.

3. Buyer Signals

- Verbal Signals: Verbal cues such as asking about next steps, inquiring about the final price, or expressing a desire to proceed are strong indicators that the buyer is ready to close.

- Non-Verbal Signals: Positive body language, such as nodding, maintaining eye contact, and showing excitement, can signal that the buyer is prepared to finalize the deal.

- Behavioral Signals: Actions such as requesting a contract, asking for implementation details, or discussing payment options suggest that the buyer is ready to close.

Strategies for Timing the Perfect Close

1. Monitor Buyer Engagement

- Track Interactions: Use CRM tools to track the buyer's interactions with your sales materials, website, and communications. Increased engagement with key content, such as pricing or product specifications, can indicate readiness.

- Assess Interest Levels: Evaluate the buyer's level of interest based on their questions, feedback, and overall engagement. A high level of interest often signifies that the buyer is close to making a decision.

2. Identify Key Decision-Making Milestones

- Understand the Buyer's Timeline: Gain insight into the buyer's decision-making timeline and any critical milestones. Timing the close to align with these milestones ensures that you are addressing their needs at the right moment.

- Confirm Budget and Approval Status: Verify that the buyer has the necessary budget and internal approvals before attempting to close. Address any financial or approval-related concerns in advance to facilitate a smooth closing process.

3. Use Trial Closes

- Gauge Readiness: Employ trial closes to gauge the buyer's readiness to move forward. Phrases like "How does this solution align with your needs?" or "What do you think about the proposed terms?" help assess their level of commitment.

- Address Concerns: Use trial closes to identify and address any remaining concerns or objections. This helps ensure that all issues are resolved before moving to the final close.

4. Tailor Your Approach

- Customize the Closing Pitch: Tailor your closing pitch based on the buyer's specific needs, preferences, and signals. Highlight the key benefits and value propositions that align with their priorities.

- Provide Reassurance: Offer reassurance and address any last-minute concerns to build confidence and reinforce the decision to proceed. Emphasize the positive outcomes and benefits of making the purchase.

5. Create a Sense of Urgency

- Highlight Limited Offers: If applicable, emphasize any limited-time offers, discounts, or promotions to create a sense of urgency. This can motivate the buyer to take action and finalize the deal.

- Set Clear Deadlines: Establish clear deadlines for making a decision or completing the purchase. Setting deadlines helps create a sense of urgency and encourages the buyer to act promptly.

6. Prepare for the Close

- Have Documentation Ready: Ensure that all necessary documentation, such as contracts or agreements, is prepared and ready for the closing process. Having these materials in place facilitates a smooth and efficient close.

- Plan the Next Steps: Clearly outline the next steps in the process, including any follow-up actions, implementation plans, or post-sale support. Providing a clear path forward helps guide the buyer through the final stages of the sale.

Best Practices for Executing the Close

1. Be Direct and Confident

- Clearly Ask for the Sale: When the timing is right, confidently ask for the sale. Phrases like "Are you ready to proceed with the purchase?" or "Shall we move forward with the agreement?" clearly signal that you are ready to close.

- Maintain Professionalism: Approach the close with professionalism and confidence. A positive and assertive attitude reassures the buyer and reinforces their decision to proceed.

2. Address Last-Minute Concerns

- Resolve Issues Promptly: If the buyer raises any last-minute concerns or objections, address them promptly and effectively. Ensuring that all issues are resolved before closing helps prevent delays and reinforces the buyer's confidence.

- Provide Final Reassurance: Offer final reassurance and emphasize the benefits of the purchase to reinforce the buyer's decision. Highlight how the solution will meet their needs and deliver positive outcomes.

3. Confirm the Details

- Review Terms and Conditions: Clearly review and confirm the terms and conditions of the sale, including pricing, payment terms, delivery schedules, and any other relevant details. Ensuring that both parties are aligned on these details helps avoid misunderstandings.

- Obtain Signatures: Secure any necessary signatures or approvals to finalize the sale. Ensure that all documentation is completed accurately and promptly to complete the transaction.

Conclusion

Timing the perfect close is a critical skill in sales that involves recognizing the right moment to finalize a deal and executing the close with confidence. By understanding the factors influencing timing, monitoring buyer engagement, identifying key decision-making milestones, and employing effective closing strategies, sales professionals can increase their chances of successfully closing deals.

Executing the close involves being direct and confident, addressing last-minute concerns, and confirming all details to ensure a smooth and successful transaction. Mastering the art of timing the perfect close not only enhances sales success but also strengthens relationships with buyers by providing a positive and satisfying experience.

Essential Closing Techniques for Every Salesperson

In sales, closing techniques are critical for converting prospects into customers. Effective closing techniques help sales professionals navigate the final stages of the sales process, address buyer concerns, and secure commitments. Mastering these techniques can significantly enhance a salesperson's ability to close deals and drive business success. This essay outlines essential closing techniques every salesperson should master, including the assumptive close, summary close, alternative close, urgency close, and direct close.

1. The Assumptive Close

Overview: The assumptive close operates on the premise that the prospect has already decided to make a purchase. This technique involves moving forward with the sales process as if the decision to buy has been made.

How It Works:
- Assume the Sale: Proceed with steps such as finalizing the contract, discussing delivery details, or arranging payment options as if the prospect has already committed.
- Positive Language: Use positive, future-oriented language to reinforce the assumption. For example, "Let's go ahead and set up the delivery date for next week."

Benefits:
- Encourages Commitment: By acting as if the sale is already closed, you can guide the prospect smoothly toward finalizing the deal.
- Builds Confidence: Demonstrates confidence in the product and the prospect's decision, which can positively influence their commitment.

Tips for Success:
- Gauge Readiness: Ensure that the prospect has shown clear signs of readiness before using this technique. The assumptive close works best when the prospect is already interested and engaged.

2. The Summary Close

Overview: The summary close involves recapping the key benefits and value propositions of the product or service to reinforce the prospect's decision to buy.

How It Works:
- Summarize Key Points: Recap the main benefits and features that address the prospect's needs and concerns. For example, "To summarize, our solution offers [benefits] that will help you [solve specific problem]."
- Confirm Readiness: After summarizing, ask if the prospect is ready to proceed. For example, "Does this summary align with what you're looking for? Are you ready to move forward?"

Benefits:
- Reinforces Value: Helps the prospect remember the key reasons they were interested in the first place and reinforces the value of the product or service.
- Addresses Concerns: Provides an opportunity to address any final questions or concerns the prospect might have.

Tips for Success:
- Be Concise: Keep the summary focused on the most important benefits and avoid overwhelming the prospect with too much detail.
- Tailor the Summary: Customize the summary to reflect the specific needs and priorities of the prospect.

3. The Alternative Close

Overview: The alternative close offers the prospect a choice between two or more options, guiding them toward a decision by focusing on how they want to proceed rather than whether they want to buy.

How It Works:
- Present Options: Offer two or more choices, such as different packages, payment plans, or product features. For example, "Would you prefer the standard package or the premium option?"

- Guide Decision-Making: Use the options to steer the prospect toward making a decision. For example, "Which option works best for you?"

Benefits:

- Reduces Pressure: Shifts the focus from a binary decision (buy or not buy) to selecting between options, which can be less intimidating for the prospect.
- Encourages Commitment: Helps the prospect make a choice and commit to the next step.

Tips for Success:

- Provide Clear Choices: Ensure that the options you offer are clear and relevant to the prospect's needs.
- Avoid Overloading: Limit the number of options to avoid overwhelming the prospect.

4. The Urgency Close

Overview: The urgency close creates a sense of urgency to encourage the prospect to make a decision quickly. This technique leverages time-sensitive factors to motivate action.

How It Works:

- Highlight Time-Sensitive Elements: Emphasize factors such as limited-time offers, upcoming price increases, or product availability. For example, "This discount is only available until the end of the month."
- Stress Benefits of Immediate Action: Explain the benefits of acting now, such as securing the best price or receiving faster delivery. For example, "By signing up today, you'll receive expedited shipping at no extra cost."

Benefits:

- Motivates Action: Creates a sense of urgency that can prompt the prospect to make a decision sooner.
- Leverages Scarcity: Uses scarcity and time constraints to increase the perceived value of the offer.

Tips for Success:

- Be Honest: Ensure that the urgency is genuine and not misleading. Overstating urgency can damage trust and harm the relationship.

- Balance Urgency with Support: While creating urgency, continue to offer support and address any remaining concerns.

5. The Direct Close

Overview: The direct close involves asking the prospect directly for the sale. This straightforward approach seeks a clear commitment from the prospect.

How It Works:
- Ask for the Sale: Pose a direct question to the prospect, such as "Are you ready to proceed with the purchase?" or "Can we finalize the agreement today?"
- Be Clear and Confident: Communicate clearly and confidently, making it easy for the prospect to make a decision.

Benefits:
- Simplicity: Provides a straightforward approach that eliminates ambiguity and confusion.
- Encourages Decision-Making: Directly prompts the prospect to make a decision, which can be effective if they are already interested and engaged.

Tips for Success:
- Ensure Readiness: Use the direct close when the prospect has shown clear signs of readiness and is likely to commit.
- Maintain Professionalism: Approach the direct close with professionalism and respect, ensuring that the prospect feels comfortable with the decision-making process.

Conclusion

Mastering essential closing techniques is crucial for sales professionals aiming to convert prospects into customers successfully. The assumptive close, summary close, alternative close, urgency close, and direct close each offer unique advantages and can be applied based on the prospect's needs and stage in the decision-making process.

By understanding and effectively utilizing these techniques, salespeople can enhance their ability to close deals, build stronger customer relationships, and drive business success. Successful closing involves not only employing the right techniques but also being attentive to the prospect's signals and needs throughout the sales process.

Customising Your Approach for Different Client Types

In sales, recognizing and adapting to different client types is crucial for maximizing engagement, addressing unique needs, and achieving successful outcomes. Customizing your approach ensures that you are effectively meeting each client's expectations and preferences. This essay explores strategies for tailoring your sales approach to different client types, including the analytical client, the amiable client, the driver client, and the expressive client. By understanding these client types and adjusting your approach accordingly, sales professionals can enhance their effectiveness and build stronger client relationships.

1. The Analytical Client

Characteristics:
- Data-Driven: Analytical clients prioritize data, facts, and detailed information. They make decisions based on thorough analysis and logical reasoning.
- Detail-Oriented: They appreciate comprehensive explanations and clear evidence supporting claims.
- Risk-Averse: They are cautious and prefer to minimize risks by evaluating all available information before making a decision.

Customizing Your Approach:
- Provide Detailed Information: Offer thorough and precise details about your product or service. Use data, case studies, and technical specifications to support your claims.
- Focus on ROI: Highlight the return on investment (ROI) and long-term benefits. Analytical clients are interested in how the product will impact their bottom line.
- Be Prepared for Questions: Anticipate and be ready to answer detailed questions about features, performance, and cost. Provide evidence and documentation to address their concerns.

Example: If you are selling software to an analytical client, provide them with a detailed report on the software's performance metrics, user case studies, and a cost-benefit analysis.

2. The Amiable Client

Characteristics:

- Relationship-Focused: Amiable clients value personal connections and trust. They seek harmony and prefer working with individuals who are empathetic and understanding.
- Supportive: They are often cooperative and willing to collaborate, but they may take longer to make decisions as they weigh the impact on relationships.
- Concerned with Support: They prioritize customer service and support, valuing a partnership that offers ongoing assistance.

Customizing Your Approach:

- Build Rapport: Establish a personal connection by showing empathy and understanding their needs. Engage in friendly, relationship-building conversations.
- Emphasize Support and Service: Highlight the support, training, and customer service that come with your product. Reassure them about the assistance they will receive throughout the relationship.
- Be Patient: Allow them time to make decisions and avoid pressuring them. Show that you value their comfort and are committed to their satisfaction.

Example: When selling a consulting service to an amiable client, focus on how your service will support their goals and enhance their team's effectiveness. Emphasize your commitment to their success and long-term partnership.

3. The Driver Client

Characteristics:

- Goal-Oriented: Driver clients are focused on results and efficiency. They make decisions quickly and are concerned with achieving their objectives.
- Decisive: They appreciate straightforward, concise information and expect quick responses. They value efficiency and effectiveness.

- Competitive: They are often competitive and driven by outcomes. They want to see how your product or service will give them a competitive edge.

Customizing Your Approach:

- Be Direct and Concise: Provide clear, to-the-point information that highlights how your product or service will help them achieve their goals. Avoid unnecessary details.
- Focus on Results: Emphasize the tangible results, benefits, and efficiencies your product or service offers. Highlight competitive advantages and performance metrics.
- Act Quickly: Respond promptly to their inquiries and be prepared to make decisions quickly. Show that you can deliver results efficiently.

Example: When pitching a high-performance product to a driver client, focus on its impact on productivity and competitive advantage. Provide a quick overview of the key benefits and be ready to finalize the deal swiftly.

4. The Expressive Client

Characteristics:

- Visionary: Expressive clients are enthusiastic, creative, and focused on big ideas and possibilities. They are motivated by innovation and potential.
- People-Oriented: They value relationships and are influenced by the salesperson's personality and energy.
- Innovative: They are interested in new ideas and approaches and are often willing to take risks for potential rewards.

Customizing Your Approach:

- Show Enthusiasm: Match their energy and enthusiasm. Share your excitement about the product or service and how it can impact their vision and goals.
- Focus on Innovation: Highlight the innovative aspects and unique features of your product or service. Emphasize how it aligns with their creative vision and goals.
- Build a Relationship: Develop a strong personal connection by engaging in meaningful conversations and demonstrating your passion for their ideas.

Example: When presenting a new marketing strategy to an expressive client, emphasize how it can revolutionize their brand and align with their innovative vision. Share success stories and showcase creative examples.

Conclusion

Customizing your sales approach for different client types is essential for building effective relationships and achieving successful outcomes. By understanding the characteristics and preferences of analytical, amiable, driver, and expressive clients, sales professionals can tailor their strategies to meet each client's needs and expectations.

The ability to adapt your approach based on client type enhances your effectiveness in addressing their concerns, providing relevant information, and ultimately closing deals. Successful sales interactions are rooted in recognizing and respecting the unique attributes of each client, leading to stronger relationships and better business results.

The Role of Communication in Effective Closing

Effective communication is fundamental to successful sales closing. It shapes the interactions between sales professionals and prospects, influencing how well the salesperson can address needs, handle objections, and secure commitments. This essay explores the critical role of communication in the closing process, including the importance of clarity, active listening, persuasive techniques, and non-verbal cues. Mastering these aspects of communication enhances a salesperson's ability to close deals successfully and build strong client relationships.

1. Clarity in Communication

1. Clear Messaging:
- Articulate Value Propositions: Clearly convey the benefits and value propositions of the product or service. Ensure that the messaging aligns with the prospect's needs and pain points. For example, instead of saying, "Our software is user-friendly," specify, "Our software reduces training time by 50% and has a 98% user satisfaction rate."
- Simplify Complex Information: Break down complex information into easy-to-understand terms. Use simple language and avoid jargon that might confuse the prospect.

2. Avoiding Ambiguity:
- Be Direct and Specific: Ensure that all communications are direct and specific. Ambiguity can lead to misunderstandings or hesitations. For instance, clearly state the terms of the offer, pricing details, and next steps.
- Confirm Understanding: Regularly check that the prospect understands the information provided. Ask questions like, "Does this explanation make sense?" or "Do you have any questions about this aspect?"

3. Consistent Messaging:
- Align with Marketing Materials: Ensure that your verbal communication aligns with any marketing materials or written proposals. Inconsistencies can create confusion and erode trust.
- Maintain Consistency: Be consistent in the messages you convey throughout the sales process, including follow-ups and final negotiations.

2. Active Listening

1. Understanding Needs:

- Ask Open-Ended Questions: Use open-ended questions to encourage prospects to share their needs, preferences, and concerns. For example, "Can you tell me more about the challenges you're facing with your current solution?"
- Listen More Than You Speak: Allow the prospect to speak freely, and listen attentively to understand their requirements and objections.

2. Reflecting and Clarifying:

- Paraphrase and Summarize: Reflect on what the prospect has said by paraphrasing or summarizing their points. This demonstrates that you have heard and understood their needs. For example, "So, you're looking for a solution that can integrate with your existing systems and improve efficiency, is that correct?"
- Seek Confirmation: Confirm your understanding by asking follow-up questions or seeking validation. This helps ensure that you are addressing the right issues and provides clarity.

3. Demonstrating Empathy:

- Show Genuine Interest: Express empathy by acknowledging the prospect's concerns and showing that you understand their perspective. For instance, "I understand that cost is a significant factor for you. Let's explore some options that fit within your budget."

3. Persuasive Techniques

1. Tailored Solutions:

- Customize Your Approach: Tailor your presentation and responses to address the specific needs and preferences of the prospect. Use information gathered during the conversation to offer customized solutions.
- Highlight Benefits and ROI: Emphasize how your product or service will meet the prospect's needs and deliver a return on investment. Use persuasive language to illustrate the benefits clearly.

2. Overcoming Objections:

- Address Concerns Directly: Handle objections by providing clear and compelling responses. Use evidence, testimonials, or case studies to counter objections and reinforce the value of your offering.
- Stay Positive and Confident: Maintain a positive and confident tone when addressing objections. Your demeanor can influence the prospect's perception and help resolve concerns more effectively.

3. Using Persuasive Language:

- Frame Benefits Positively: Use positive language to frame the benefits and advantages of your product or service. For example, instead of "This software is less expensive than our competitors," say "This software offers exceptional value at a competitive price."
- Encourage Action: Use call-to-action phrases that encourage the prospect to take the next step. For example, "Let's go ahead and finalize the agreement so you can start benefiting from our solution immediately."

4. Non-Verbal Communication

1. Body Language:
- Maintain Open Posture: Use open and welcoming body language to create a positive and approachable atmosphere. Avoid crossing your arms or appearing closed off.
- Use Gestures: Employ appropriate gestures to emphasize key points and show enthusiasm. For example, nodding while listening demonstrates engagement and agreement.

2. Eye Contact:
- Establish Connection: Maintain eye contact to build trust and demonstrate confidence. Avoiding eye contact can create a sense of disconnection or unease.
- Gauge Reactions: Observe the prospect's eye contact and body language to gauge their level of interest and engagement. Adjust your approach based on their non-verbal cues.

3. Tone and Pace:
- Match Tone to Context: Adjust your tone of voice to match the context of the conversation. Use a calm and reassuring tone when addressing concerns, and a confident and enthusiastic tone when discussing benefits.

- Control Pace: Maintain a pace that matches the prospect's communication style. Avoid rushing through the closing process or speaking too slowly.

Conclusion

Effective communication plays a pivotal role in closing sales successfully. By ensuring clarity in messaging, practicing active listening, employing persuasive techniques, and being mindful of non-verbal communication, sales professionals can significantly enhance their ability to close deals and build lasting relationships with clients.

Mastering these aspects of communication allows salespeople to address client needs, handle objections, and guide prospects toward making informed decisions. Ultimately, successful closing is achieved through clear, empathetic, and persuasive communication that aligns with the prospect's needs and preferences.

Handling Rejections and Turning Nos into Yeses

In sales, rejection is an inevitable part of the process. However, how you handle rejections can significantly impact your success and growth. Learning to turn "nos" into "yeses" involves understanding the reasons behind the rejection, addressing concerns effectively, and maintaining a positive and resilient attitude. This essay explores strategies for handling rejections and converting objections into opportunities for closing deals.

1. Understanding the Rejection

1. Analyze the Reason:
- Seek Feedback: When a prospect rejects your offer, ask for feedback to understand their reasons. Questions like, "Can you share why you've decided not to move forward?" can provide valuable insights.
- Identify Patterns: Look for common themes in the reasons for rejection. This can help you identify areas for improvement in your approach or offering.

2. Assess the Timing:
- Evaluate the Timing: Sometimes, a rejection is due to timing rather than the product or service itself. For example, a prospect may not be ready to purchase due to budget constraints or competing priorities.
- Follow Up Later: If timing is an issue, set a reminder to follow up at a later date. Revisit the conversation when the prospect's circumstances change.

3. Maintain Professionalism:
- Stay Positive: Approach rejection with professionalism and positivity. Avoid taking it personally and focus on learning from the experience.
- Respect Their Decision: Respect the prospect's decision and avoid being pushy. Demonstrating respect can leave the door open for future opportunities.

2. Addressing Concerns Effectively

1. Reframe the Conversation:

- Acknowledge Concerns: Address the prospect's concerns directly. For example, if price is a concern, explain the value and return on investment that justifies the cost.
- Provide Solutions: Offer solutions or alternatives that address the prospect's objections. For instance, if the issue is budget, suggest a different payment plan or a scaled-down version of the product.

2. Highlight Value:

- Emphasize Benefits: Reiterate the key benefits and value propositions of your product or service. Show how it solves the prospect's specific problems or meets their needs.
- Use Testimonials: Share success stories or testimonials from other clients who have faced similar concerns. This can help build credibility and demonstrate that your offering delivers results.

3. Offer Additional Information:

- Provide More Details: If the prospect is hesitant due to lack of information, offer additional details or resources. This might include case studies, product demos, or detailed explanations.
- Clarify Misunderstandings: Clear up any misunderstandings or misconceptions that may have contributed to the rejection.

3. Building Resilience and Persistence

1. Develop a Positive Attitude:

- Focus on Learning: View rejection as an opportunity to learn and improve. Reflect on what went well and what could be adjusted in your approach.
- Stay Motivated: Maintain a positive mindset and keep your motivation high. Persistence and resilience are key to overcoming setbacks and achieving success.

2. Practice Active Listening:

- Listen to Feedback: Pay close attention to the feedback provided by the prospect. Use it to refine your approach and better understand client needs.

- Adapt and Improve: Continuously adapt your sales strategies based on feedback and experiences. Improvement and growth come from understanding and addressing challenges.

3. Build Relationships:
- Nurture Relationships: Maintain relationships with prospects who have rejected your offer. Stay in touch and provide value through useful content, updates, or industry insights.
- Create Future Opportunities: By building and nurturing relationships, you increase the likelihood of future opportunities. A prospect who initially said no may become interested later as their needs evolve.

4. Turning Objections into Opportunities

1. Follow-Up Strategies:
- Schedule Follow-Ups: Set up follow-up meetings or calls to stay connected with the prospect. Use this time to provide additional value or discuss new developments.
- Personalize Communication: Tailor your follow-up communication to address the specific reasons for the initial rejection. Show that you have considered their feedback and made relevant adjustments.

2. Offer Value Beyond the Sale:
- Provide Additional Resources: Offer valuable resources, such as industry reports or helpful tips, to keep the prospect engaged and build trust.
- Show Continued Interest: Demonstrate that you are genuinely interested in helping the prospect, even if they have not yet committed to a purchase.

3. Reassess Your Approach:
- Refine Your Pitch: Use insights from rejections to refine and enhance your sales pitch. Tailor your approach based on what you have learned about the prospect's needs and preferences.
- Adjust Your Offerings: Consider making adjustments to your product or service based on feedback received. This can make your offering more appealing to future prospects.

Conclusion

Handling rejections effectively and turning "nos" into "yeses" requires a combination of understanding, resilience, and strategic adaptation. By analyzing the reasons behind rejections, addressing concerns with tailored solutions, maintaining a positive attitude, and leveraging follow-up opportunities, sales professionals can transform setbacks into opportunities for growth and success.

Rejection is an inherent part of the sales process, but how you respond can determine your overall success. Embracing rejection as a learning experience and continuously refining your approach can lead to improved sales outcomes and stronger client relationships.

Leveraging Technology to Improve Closing Rates

In today's competitive sales environment, leveraging technology can significantly enhance the efficiency and effectiveness of the closing process. Advanced tools and systems offer valuable insights, streamline workflows, and provide data-driven strategies to improve closing rates. This essay explores key technological tools and strategies that sales professionals can use to boost their closing rates, including customer relationship management (CRM) systems, sales automation tools, data analytics, and digital communication platforms.

1. Customer Relationship Management (CRM) Systems

1. Centralized Data Management:
- Track Interactions: CRM systems enable sales teams to track and manage all interactions with prospects and customers in a centralized database. This includes contact information, meeting notes, email correspondence, and purchase history.
- Access to Insights: Sales professionals can access detailed insights into client behavior, preferences, and past interactions. This helps in tailoring communication and offers based on historical data.

2. Improved Follow-Up:
- Automated Reminders: CRMs can automate reminders for follow-up activities, ensuring that sales reps stay on top of their engagements and don't miss opportunities for timely follow-ups.
- Scheduled Communication: Sales professionals can schedule follow-up emails and calls, maintaining consistent communication without manual intervention.

3. Enhanced Collaboration:
- Team Coordination: CRMs facilitate better collaboration among sales team members by providing a shared platform for updating client information and sharing notes.
- Reporting and Analytics: CRM systems generate reports on sales performance, pipeline status, and lead conversion rates, helping teams analyze and refine their strategies.

Example: Salesforce and HubSpot CRM are popular platforms that offer extensive features for managing client interactions, automating tasks, and analyzing sales data.

2. Sales Automation Tools

1. Automated Outreach:

- Email Sequencing: Sales automation tools allow for the creation of automated email sequences that nurture leads through the sales funnel. These sequences can be customized based on the prospect's behavior and engagement level.

- Follow-Up Automation: Automate follow-up emails and reminders based on predefined triggers, such as after a meeting or when a lead exhibits specific behaviors.

2. Streamlined Processes:

- Proposal Generation: Automation tools can generate proposals and contracts quickly using pre-set templates, reducing the time spent on manual document creation and increasing efficiency.

- Lead Scoring: Automate lead scoring based on criteria such as engagement level, company size, or purchase intent, helping sales teams prioritize high-potential leads.

3. Integration with CRM:

- Seamless Integration: Sales automation tools often integrate with CRM systems, allowing for synchronized data and streamlined processes. This integration helps ensure that all client interactions and data are up-to-date and accessible.

Example: Tools like Outreach and SalesLoft offer automation features for email sequencing, follow-ups, and lead scoring, helping sales teams enhance their outreach efforts and close more deals.

3. Data Analytics and Insights

1. Sales Performance Analysis:

- Track Metrics: Data analytics tools allow sales teams to track key performance metrics such as conversion rates, average deal size, and sales cycle length. Analyzing these metrics provides insights into areas of improvement.
- Predictive Analytics: Utilize predictive analytics to forecast future sales trends and identify patterns that can inform strategic decisions. This helps in anticipating client needs and adjusting sales tactics accordingly.

2. Customer Insights:
- Behavioral Analysis: Analyze customer behavior data to understand their preferences, buying patterns, and pain points. This information can be used to tailor sales pitches and address specific client needs.
- Segmentation: Segment your customer base based on various criteria such as industry, company size, or engagement level. This allows for more targeted and personalized sales approaches.

3. Data-Driven Decision Making:
- Informed Strategies: Use data-driven insights to refine sales strategies, optimize lead generation efforts, and improve closing techniques. Make decisions based on empirical evidence rather than intuition alone.

Example: Google Analytics and Tableau are powerful tools for analyzing sales performance and customer behavior, providing actionable insights for improving closing rates.

4. Digital Communication Platforms

1. Virtual Meetings:
- Online Conferencing: Tools like Zoom and Microsoft Teams facilitate virtual meetings and presentations, allowing sales professionals to connect with prospects and clients regardless of location.
- Screen Sharing: Use screen sharing to present product demos, walkthroughs, and proposals in real-time, enhancing engagement and providing a more interactive experience.

2. Instant Messaging:
- Real-Time Communication: Platforms like Slack or Microsoft Teams enable real-time communication with clients and team members. Instant messaging can help address questions and concerns quickly, improving the overall sales experience.

- Collaboration: Facilitate collaboration with internal teams by sharing updates, documents, and feedback through messaging platforms, ensuring that everyone is aligned on client interactions and strategies.

3. Enhanced Engagement:
- Personalized Interactions: Use digital communication tools to personalize interactions based on client preferences and engagement history. Tailor your communication style and content to match the prospect's needs.

Example: Zoom and Slack are widely used for virtual meetings and real-time communication, helping sales professionals stay connected and responsive to client needs.

Conclusion

Leveraging technology is essential for improving closing rates and enhancing the overall effectiveness of the sales process. By utilizing CRM systems, sales automation tools, data analytics, and digital communication platforms, sales professionals can streamline their workflows, gain valuable insights, and engage clients more effectively.

Technology not only simplifies and accelerates various aspects of the sales process but also provides the tools needed for data-driven decision-making and personalized client interactions. Embracing these technological advancements can lead to more successful closes, stronger client relationships, and increased sales performance.

Case Studies of Successful Sales Closings

Case studies offer valuable insights into successful sales strategies and practices that can be applied to improve sales closing rates. By examining real-world examples, sales professionals can learn from best practices, understand different approaches, and adapt strategies to their own contexts. Below are three case studies highlighting different aspects of successful sales closings.

Case Study 1: HubSpot's Inbound Sales Strategy

Background:
HubSpot, a leading provider of marketing, sales, and service software, faced the challenge of scaling its sales operations while maintaining a high level of personalization and effectiveness.

Strategy Implemented:
1. Inbound Sales Approach:
   - HubSpot adopted an inbound sales strategy, focusing on attracting, engaging, and delighting prospects through valuable content and personalized interactions.
   - The company used its own CRM system to track leads and analyze their interactions with content, enabling a deeper understanding of prospect needs.

2. Lead Nurturing:
   - HubSpot implemented automated lead nurturing workflows, using targeted email campaigns and personalized content to guide prospects through the sales funnel.
   - Sales reps were equipped with tools to track prospect engagement and tailor their outreach based on the prospect's interests and behavior.

3. Data-Driven Insights:
   - HubSpot utilized data analytics to monitor lead performance, measure the effectiveness of different sales tactics, and identify trends in customer behavior.

- Insights gained from data were used to refine sales strategies and improve targeting.

Outcome:

- Increased Efficiency: HubSpot's inbound sales strategy led to a significant increase in lead conversion rates and reduced the time required to close deals.

- Higher Engagement: Personalized and relevant content improved engagement and trust with prospects, leading to more successful closes.

- Scalable Growth: The use of automation and data analytics allowed HubSpot to scale its sales operations effectively while maintaining a high level of personalization.

Case Study 2: IBM's Solution Selling Approach

Background:
IBM faced challenges in selling complex enterprise solutions to large organizations. The company needed to improve its ability to close high-value deals in a highly competitive market.

Strategy Implemented:
1. Solution Selling:
   - IBM adopted a solution selling approach, focusing on understanding the unique needs and pain points of each client and offering tailored solutions rather than generic products.
   - Sales teams were trained to engage in consultative selling, working closely with clients to design solutions that addressed their specific challenges.

2. Customer-Centric Approach:
   - IBM emphasized building long-term relationships with clients by providing value beyond the initial sale. This included offering ongoing support, customized services, and strategic insights.
   - The company used its CRM system to track client interactions and preferences, ensuring that sales reps could deliver personalized recommendations.

3. Collaborative Engagement:

- IBM fostered collaboration between sales, product development, and client services teams to ensure that solutions were well-aligned with client needs and delivered effectively.

Outcome:

- Increased Deal Size: IBM's solution selling approach resulted in larger and more complex deals, as the company was able to address specific client needs with tailored solutions.
- Stronger Relationships: By focusing on client relationships and providing ongoing value, IBM built trust and loyalty, leading to repeat business and referrals.
- Competitive Advantage: The consultative approach and customized solutions differentiated IBM from competitors and enhanced its position in the market.

Case Study 3: Salesforce's Data-Driven Sales Strategies

Background:
Salesforce, a global leader in CRM solutions, aimed to improve its sales closing rates and optimise its sales processes.

Strategy Implemented:
1. Data Analytics:
   - Salesforce leveraged its own CRM and analytics tools to gain insights into sales performance, prospect behaviour, and market trends.
   - The company used predictive analytics to identify high-potential leads and prioritise them based on their likelihood to convert.

2. Sales Enablement:
   - Salesforce implemented sales enablement tools to provide sales reps with real-time data, sales collateral, and training resources. This helped reps engage prospects more effectively and close deals more efficiently.
   - The company used its CRM system to automate routine tasks, such as follow-up reminders and meeting scheduling, allowing sales reps to focus on high-value activities.

3. Continuous Improvement:

   - Salesforce emphasised continuous improvement by regularly reviewing sales performance data, gathering feedback from sales teams, and iterating on sales strategies and processes.

Outcome:

- Improved Closing Rates: Salesforce's data-driven approach led to higher closing rates by enabling sales reps to focus on the most promising leads and use insights to tailor their sales pitches.
- Enhanced Productivity: Automation and sales enablement tools increased sales rep productivity, allowing them to close more deals in less time.
- Data-Driven Decision Making: The use of data analytics provided valuable insights that informed strategic decisions and refined sales tactics.

Conclusion

These case studies demonstrate that successful sales closings often involve a combination of tailored strategies, technology utilisation, and a deep understanding of client needs. HubSpot's inbound sales strategy highlights the importance of personalised engagement and automation. IBM's solution selling approach underscores the value of consultative selling and building long-term client relationships. Salesforce's data-driven strategies showcase the impact of leveraging technology and analytics to optimise sales processes.

By learning from these real-world examples, sales professionals can adopt and adapt strategies that enhance their own sales performance, improve closing rates, and build stronger client relationships.

Measuring and Improving Your Closing Success

Measuring and improving closing success is crucial for enhancing sales performance and achieving business goals. Effective measurement helps identify strengths and weaknesses in the sales process, while continuous improvement strategies ensure that sales teams adapt and refine their techniques for better outcomes. This essay outlines key metrics for measuring closing success and provides strategies for ongoing improvement.

1. Key Metrics for Measuring Closing Success

1. Close Rate (Conversion Rate):
- Definition: The close rate, or conversion rate, is the percentage of leads or prospects that are successfully converted into customers. It is calculated as the number of closed deals divided by the total number of leads or opportunities.
- Importance: This metric provides insight into the effectiveness of the sales process and the ability to close deals. A higher close rate indicates successful sales tactics and effective lead management.

2. Average Deal Size:
- Definition: Average deal size is the average revenue generated per closed deal. It is calculated by dividing the total revenue from closed deals by the number of deals.
- Importance: This metric helps assess the value of deals being closed and the effectiveness of upselling or cross-selling strategies. It also provides insights into pricing strategies and market positioning.

3. Sales Cycle Length:
- Definition: Sales cycle length is the average time it takes to close a deal from the initial contact to finalizing the sale. It is measured in days or weeks.
- Importance: This metric indicates the efficiency of the sales process and helps identify bottlenecks or delays. A shorter sales cycle often reflects a streamlined process and effective sales techniques.

4. Lead-to-Close Ratio:

- Definition: The lead-to-close ratio measures the number of leads required to close a deal. It is calculated by dividing the number of leads by the number of closed deals.
- Importance: This metric helps evaluate the quality of leads and the effectiveness of lead qualification and nurturing processes. A lower lead-to-close ratio indicates better lead quality and more efficient sales efforts.

5. Win-Loss Ratio:
- Definition: The win-loss ratio compares the number of deals won to the number of deals lost. It is calculated as the number of won deals divided by the number of lost deals.
- Importance: This metric provides insights into the competitiveness of the sales process and the effectiveness of closing techniques. It helps identify areas for improvement and assess overall sales performance.

2. Strategies for Improving Closing Success

1. Analyse Sales Data:
- Identify Trends: Regularly analyse sales data to identify trends and patterns in closing success. Look for correlations between successful deals and factors such as lead sources, sales techniques, and client characteristics.
- Assess Performance: Evaluate individual and team performance based on key metrics. Identify high-performing sales reps and analyse their techniques to replicate success across the team.

2. Enhance Sales Training:
- Skills Development: Provide ongoing training to sales reps to improve their closing skills, including negotiation, objection handling, and relationship building. Use role-playing and real-world scenarios to practise and refine techniques.
- Knowledge Sharing: Encourage knowledge sharing among sales team members. Hold regular meetings or workshops where top performers can share their strategies and best practices.

3. Refine Sales Processes:
- Streamline Workflows: Identify and eliminate inefficiencies in the sales process. Simplify workflows, automate routine tasks, and ensure that sales reps have access to the tools and resources they need.

- Improve Lead Qualification: Enhance lead qualification processes to ensure that sales reps focus on high-potential leads. Use lead scoring and segmentation to prioritise leads based on their likelihood to convert.

4. Implement Effective Sales Tools:

- CRM Systems: Use CRM systems to track and manage leads, opportunities, and client interactions. CRM tools provide valuable data and insights that can help optimise sales strategies and improve closing success.

- Sales Automation: Implement sales automation tools to streamline tasks such as follow-up emails, appointment scheduling, and proposal generation. Automation frees up time for sales reps to focus on high-value activities.

5. Focus on Client Relationships:

- Build Trust: Develop strong relationships with clients by demonstrating genuine interest in their needs and providing valuable solutions. Building trust increases the likelihood of closing deals and fosters long-term loyalty.

- Address Objections: Effectively handle client objections by understanding their concerns and offering solutions. Address objections with empathy and provide clear, compelling responses to overcome barriers to closing.

6. Continuously Monitor and Adapt:

- Track Progress: Regularly monitor key metrics and assess progress toward sales goals. Use performance data to make informed decisions and adjust strategies as needed.

- Solicit Feedback: Gather feedback from clients and sales team members to identify areas for improvement. Use this feedback to refine sales approaches and enhance overall effectiveness.

7. Utilise Technology for Insights:

- Analytics Tools: Leverage analytics tools to gain deeper insights into sales performance, customer behaviour, and market trends. Use data-driven insights to make strategic decisions and improve closing techniques.

- AI and Predictive Analytics: Implement AI and predictive analytics to forecast sales trends, identify high-potential leads, and optimise sales strategies. AI-driven insights can help tailor approaches and increase closing success.

Conclusion

Measuring and improving closing success is essential for achieving sales objectives and driving business growth. By focusing on key metrics such as close rate, average deal size, sales cycle length, lead-to-close ratio, and win-loss ratio, sales professionals can gain valuable insights into their performance and identify areas for improvement.

Implementing strategies such as analysing sales data, enhancing sales training, refining sales processes, using effective sales tools, focusing on client relationships, continuously monitoring progress, and leveraging technology can significantly boost closing success. Embracing these practices helps sales teams optimise their performance, close more deals, and achieve greater success in a competitive market.

Developing a Continuous Improvement Mindset

A continuous improvement mindset is essential for personal and organisational growth. It involves consistently seeking ways to enhance processes, skills, and performance to achieve better results over time. Cultivating this mindset requires a commitment to learning, adaptability, and a proactive approach to problem-solving. This essay explores the key components of developing a continuous improvement mindset and provides practical strategies for fostering this mindset in individuals and teams.

1. Embrace a Growth Orientation

1. Value Learning:
- Seek Knowledge: Approach challenges and opportunities with a curiosity to learn. View mistakes and failures as learning experiences rather than setbacks.
- Pursue Education: Invest in ongoing education and professional development. Attend workshops, courses, and conferences to stay updated with industry trends and best practices.

2. Cultivate Resilience:
- Adaptability: Be open to change and willing to adjust strategies based on new information or feedback. Flexibility is crucial for navigating evolving environments and improving performance.
- Perseverance: Maintain determination and perseverance in the face of obstacles. Embrace challenges as opportunities to develop new skills and solutions.

2. Foster a Culture of Feedback and Reflection

1. Encourage Feedback:
- Solicit Input: Actively seek feedback from peers, mentors, and clients to gain different perspectives on performance and areas for improvement.
- Create a Feedback Loop: Implement regular feedback mechanisms, such as performance reviews or team meetings, to facilitate open and constructive discussions.

2. Reflect on Experiences:

- Analyse Outcomes: Reflect on completed projects, successful and unsuccessful outcomes, to identify lessons learned and areas for improvement.

- Continuous Self-Assessment: Regularly assess your own performance and progress toward goals. Use this self-reflection to set new objectives and strategies.

3. Implement Systematic Approaches

1. Utilise Improvement Frameworks:

- Lean and Six Sigma: Apply frameworks like Lean and Six Sigma to identify inefficiencies, streamline processes, and enhance quality. These methodologies provide structured approaches to problem-solving and process improvement.

- Plan-Do-Check-Act (PDCA): Use the PDCA cycle to plan changes, implement them, evaluate their impact, and act on the results. This iterative process helps in making incremental improvements.

2. Set Measurable Goals:

- Define Objectives: Establish clear, measurable goals for improvement. Use metrics and key performance indicators (KPIs) to track progress and evaluate success.

- Monitor Progress: Regularly review performance against set goals and adjust strategies as needed. This ensures that efforts are aligned with desired outcomes and targets.

4. Promote Collaboration and Innovation

1. Encourage Team Collaboration:

- Share Ideas: Foster an environment where team members feel comfortable sharing ideas and suggestions for improvement. Collaborative brainstorming can lead to innovative solutions and process enhancements.

- Cross-Functional Teams: Form cross-functional teams to tackle complex problems and gain diverse perspectives. Collaboration across departments can lead to more comprehensive and effective solutions.

2. Support Innovation:

- Reward Creativity: Recognize and reward innovative ideas and approaches that contribute to improvement. Encouraging creativity and experimentation can lead to valuable advancements.

- Provide Resources: Allocate resources and support for experimentation and innovation. Allow team members to test new ideas and learn from their results.

5. Develop Personal and Professional Skills

1. Focus on Skill Development:

- Identify Areas for Growth: Assess current skills and identify areas for development. Pursue training and development opportunities to enhance these skills.

- Seek Mentorship: Engage with mentors or coaches to gain guidance and support in developing new skills and improving performance.

2. Build Expertise:

- Specialise: Develop expertise in specific areas relevant to your role or industry. Deepening knowledge in particular domains can lead to more impactful contributions and improvements.

- Stay Current: Keep up with industry trends and advancements to ensure that your skills and knowledge remain relevant and valuable.

6. Implement Process Improvements

1. Streamline Processes:

- Identify Inefficiencies: Analyse existing processes to identify bottlenecks, redundancies, and areas for improvement. Streamlining processes can lead to increased efficiency and effectiveness.

- Automate Tasks: Utilise technology to automate repetitive tasks and improve workflow. Automation can reduce manual effort and minimise errors.

2. Standardise Best Practices:

- Document Procedures: Develop and document best practices and standard operating procedures (SOPs) for routine tasks. Standardisation ensures consistency and facilitates continuous improvement.
- Regular Updates: Periodically review and update procedures to incorporate new insights, technologies, and practices.

7. Encourage a Positive Attitude

1. Cultivate Optimism:
- Focus on Solutions: Maintain a solution-oriented approach when faced with challenges. Emphasise finding solutions rather than dwelling on problems.
- Celebrate Successes: Recognize and celebrate achievements and progress. Positive reinforcement boosts morale and motivation.

2. Build a Supportive Environment:
- Promote Well-Being: Support the well-being of team members by fostering a positive work environment and encouraging work-life balance. A supportive environment contributes to overall performance and improvement.
- Encourage Collaboration: Foster a collaborative and inclusive culture where team members feel valued and motivated to contribute to continuous improvement efforts.

Conclusion

Developing a continuous improvement mindset is crucial for personal and organisational success. By embracing a growth orientation, fostering a culture of feedback and reflection, implementing systematic approaches, promoting collaboration and innovation, developing skills, and maintaining a positive attitude, individuals and teams can drive ongoing enhancements and achieve better outcomes.

A continuous improvement mindset encourages learning, adaptability, and resilience, which are essential for navigating challenges and seizing opportunities. By committing to these practices, individuals and organisations can create a culture of excellence and achieve sustained success in an ever-evolving environment.

Elevating Your Sales Career Through Masterful Closing

Masterful closing is a critical component of a successful sales career. The ability to close deals effectively not only drives revenue but also builds long-term relationships with clients and enhances professional reputation. Elevating your sales career through masterful closing involves mastering key techniques, continuously improving your skills, and leveraging strategies that drive results. This essay explores how to achieve these goals and advance your sales career through exceptional closing skills.

1. Mastering Essential Closing Techniques

1. Understand the Client's Needs:
- Consultative Selling: Develop a deep understanding of your client's needs, pain points, and objectives. Engage in consultative selling to uncover these insights and tailor your approach accordingly.
- Active Listening: Practise active listening during conversations. Pay close attention to verbal and non-verbal cues to accurately gauge client concerns and preferences.

2. Build Strong Relationships:
- Trust and Credibility: Establish trust and credibility with clients by demonstrating expertise, reliability, and a genuine interest in their success. Building strong relationships increases the likelihood of closing deals.
- Personalization: Personalise your interactions by addressing clients by name, recalling past conversations, and showing empathy. Tailored communication enhances rapport and trust.

3. Implement Proven Closing Techniques:
- Assumptive Close: Use the assumptive close technique by assuming the client is ready to buy and proceeding with finalising the details. For example, you might say, "Shall we schedule the delivery date for next week?"
- Scarcity Close: Create a sense of urgency by highlighting limited availability or time-sensitive offers. For instance, "This promotion ends tomorrow, so let's get started before it expires."

- Alternative Close: Offer clients a choice between two options, both of which lead to a sale. For example, "Would you prefer the standard or premium package?"

2. Continuously Improve Your Closing Skills

1. Seek Feedback and Reflect:
- Gather Feedback: Request feedback from clients and colleagues on your closing techniques. Use their insights to identify strengths and areas for improvement.
- Reflect on Experiences: After each sales interaction, reflect on what worked well and what could be improved. Analyse both successful and unsuccessful closes to learn from each experience.

2. Invest in Professional Development:
- Training and Workshops: Attend sales training programs, workshops, and seminars to learn new techniques and stay updated with industry trends. Look for opportunities to enhance your skills through specialised training.
- Mentorship: Seek mentorship from experienced sales professionals. Learn from their experiences, seek advice, and apply their insights to your own sales approach.

3. Practice Regularly:
- Role-Playing: Engage in role-playing exercises with colleagues to practise closing techniques in a simulated environment. This helps build confidence and refine your approach.
- Real-World Application: Apply new techniques in real sales scenarios. Continuously practice and adapt based on feedback and results.

3. Leverage Strategies for Maximising Closing Success

1. Use Data and Analytics:
- Analyse Performance Metrics: Utilise data and analytics tools to track your sales performance. Review metrics such as close rates, average deal size, and sales cycle length to identify patterns and areas for improvement.

- Leverage Insights: Use insights gained from data analysis to refine your strategies and approaches. Focus on high-impact areas to enhance your closing success.

2. Implement Effective Follow-Up:

- Timely Follow-Up: Follow up promptly after initial interactions or presentations. Timely follow-ups demonstrate professionalism and keep the momentum going.

- Personalised Communication: Tailor follow-up messages based on previous interactions and client needs. Personalised communication reinforces your commitment and interest.

3. Optimise Your Sales Process:

- Streamline Workflows: Evaluate and streamline your sales processes to eliminate inefficiencies and enhance productivity. Simplify steps where possible and focus on activities that drive results.

- Automate Tasks: Utilise sales automation tools to handle routine tasks such as scheduling and follow-ups. Automation frees up time for more strategic activities and allows for a more focused approach to closing.

4. Build a Strong Professional Network

1. Network Strategically:

- Industry Connections: Build connections within your industry by attending events, joining professional associations, and participating in industry forums. Networking can lead to valuable opportunities and referrals.

- Engage on Social Media: Leverage social media platforms such as LinkedIn to connect with industry peers, share insights, and build your professional reputation.

2. Foster Relationships with Key Stakeholders:

- Influencers and Decision-Makers: Develop relationships with key influencers and decision-makers within your target market. Cultivating these relationships can open doors to new opportunities and enhance your sales efforts.

- Client Referrals: Encourage satisfied clients to refer you to others. Referral business often comes with higher trust and a greater likelihood of closing deals.

5. Demonstrate Results and Value

1. Showcase Success Stories:
- Case Studies: Share success stories and case studies that highlight how your solutions have positively impacted other clients. Demonstrating real-world results builds credibility and trust.
- Client Testimonials: Collect and showcase testimonials from satisfied clients. Positive feedback reinforces your reputation and helps build confidence with new prospects.

2. Provide Value Beyond the Sale:
- Ongoing Support: Offer continued support and value even after the sale is closed. Providing exceptional post-sale service enhances client satisfaction and encourages repeat business.
- Educational Resources: Share valuable resources and insights with clients to help them maximise the benefits of your solution. Providing ongoing value strengthens relationships and positions you as a trusted advisor.

Conclusion

Elevating your sales career through masterful closing requires a commitment to mastering essential techniques, continuously improving skills, and leveraging effective strategies. By understanding client needs, building strong relationships, and implementing proven closing techniques, you can enhance your ability to close deals successfully.

Continuously improving your skills through feedback, training, and practice, while leveraging data, optimising processes, and building a strong network, will further enhance your closing success. Demonstrating results, providing value beyond the sale, and fostering positive relationships will solidify your reputation and advance your career in sales.

Masterful closing is not only about closing deals but also about building lasting relationships and driving long-term success. By focusing on these strategies, you can elevate your sales career and achieve exceptional results.

www.ingramcontent.com/pod-product-compliance
Lightning Source LLC
Chambersburg PA
CBHW062119220526
45471CB00010B/3795